# Go Jimmy Go!

Written by
**Rob Waring** and **Maurice Jamall**

## Before You Read

to catch someone

to win

finish line

lane

meter 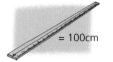 = 100cm

race

school principal

stadium

wheelchair

dangerous

second, first, third

slow

 Jimmy     Anthony     Sarah     Mark     Mr. Williams     Mr. Robert

"I'm in the 800 meter race," says a tall boy. His name is Anthony. He is writing his name on the notice.
"Which race are you in?" he asks a girl. Her name is Sarah.
"I'm in the 100 meter race, and the long jump," she says.
They are talking about Bayview High Sports Day. It is on Saturday. Everybody is excited about the races.

Anthony's friend Jimmy comes to them. Jimmy
is in a wheelchair. He loves sports very much.
"Hi, Jimmy," says Anthony. "How are you?"
"Great, thanks," says Jimmy. "Hi, Sarah," he says.
Sarah, Jimmy and Anthony talk about Sports Day.

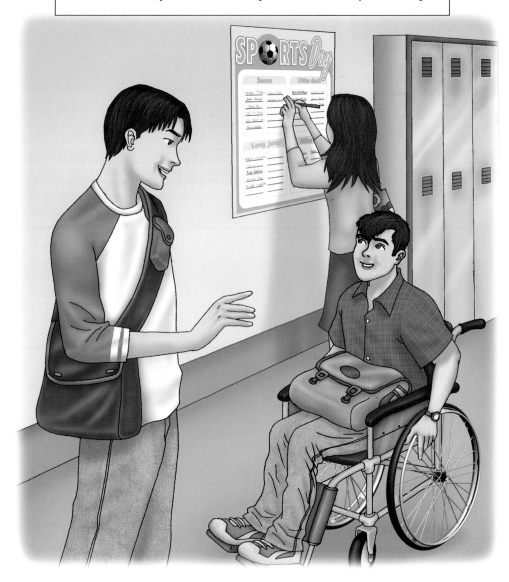

"What are you doing on Sports Day, Sarah?" he asks her.
She says, "I'm in the long jump and the 100 meter race."
"Anthony, which race are you in?" Jimmy asks.
"I'm in the 800 meter race," Anthony replies.
Jimmy says, "I'm in that race, too."

"Excuse me?" says Anthony. "Are you in the 800 meter race, Jimmy?" he asks.

"That's right. I am," replies Jimmy.

Anthony says, "Oh, but . . . but . . ." He is thinking about Jimmy and his wheelchair.

"What's wrong, Anthony?" asks Jimmy.

"Oh, umm . . . , nothing!" replies Anthony.

Sarah says, "You're in the 800 meter race. That's great, Jimmy. But be careful because Anthony's a good runner." Jimmy replies, "Yes, he's really good. I know. But I'm better than Anthony. I'm going to win."
Anthony is very surprised. He thinks, "Jimmy will never win. He's in a wheelchair!"

Later, Anthony is talking to his friend, Mark. "Mark, did you hear about Jimmy?" Anthony asks. "Jimmy's in the 800 meter race! But he's in a wheelchair! He says he's going to win!"

"Yes, I know. Jimmy's always in the 800 meter race. Jimmy's very fast, Anthony," says Mark. "He's faster than me."

Anthony is very surprised. He says, "Excuse me? Jimmy's faster than you?"

Mark replies, "Yeah, he's faster than me over 800 meters!"

The sports teacher, Mr. Williams, hears Anthony and Mark talking about Jimmy and the race.

"Excuse me, Anthony. Did you say Jimmy's in the 800 meter race?" Mr. Williams asks.

"Yes, Mr. Williams," replies Anthony.

"Oh, I see," says Mr. Williams. "Thank you." Mr. Williams walks away.

Later, Mr. Williams talks to Jimmy.

"Jimmy, Anthony says you want to be in the 800 meter race. Is that right?" asks Mr. Williams.

Jimmy replies, "Yes, that's right. I'm going to win, too!"

"I'm sorry, but you can't be in the race," says Mr. Williams.

"Why not? I want to race. Anthony can be in the race. I can, too," says Jimmy.

Mr. Williams says, "I'm sorry, but you're in a wheelchair."

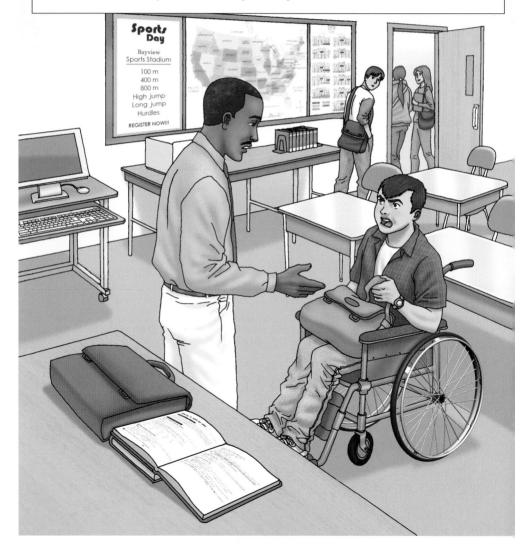

"But, Mr. Williams . . . ," says Jimmy. "I'm in a wheelchair, but I can still be in the race!"

Mr. Williams looks at Jimmy. "Your wheelchair may be dangerous to the other runners. It's too slow. You can help me start the races, or help with the . . ."

"But Mr. Williams, I *want* to race! I often race in my wheelchair," says Jimmy.

"I'm sorry, you can't be in the race," says Mr. Williams. "And don't ask again."

"But that's not fair!" says Jimmy.

Later, Jimmy sees Mark and Sarah. He tells them about the race and Mr. Williams. Jimmy is angry with Mr. Williams.

"Mr. Williams says I can't be in the 800 meter race," he tells Mark.

"Really? That's strange," says Mark. "You often race in your wheelchair."

Sarah says, "Listen, Jimmy, maybe I have an idea. You must talk to Mr. Roberts, the principal."

"Yes, I will," he says.

Later, Jimmy goes to see Mr. Roberts and Mr. Williams. Jimmy says, "Mr. Williams says I can't be in the 800 meter race. Why can't I be in the race?" he asks.

"Well . . . ," Mr. Williams replies. "It's because you're in a wheelchair. And you won't win."

Mr. Roberts says, "Mr. Williams, Jimmy just wants to be in the same race with Anthony. He doesn't want to win."

"No, Mr. Roberts! I *will* win the race!" says Jimmy.
The principal says, "That's okay. I understand.
Jimmy wants to try, and that's good."
"But . . . but . . . it's dangerous," says Mr. Williams.
"His wheelchair's dangerous for the other runners.
There may be trouble. He may fall down and hit
another runner."

Mr. Roberts asks, "How many runners are there in the race, Mr. Williams?"

"There are six runners," he answers.

Mr. Roberts asks, "Can you make two lanes only for Jimmy?"

"Well, umm . . . Yes, I think so," says Mr. Williams.

"Good," says Mr. Roberts. "So Jimmy *can* be in the race," he says to Mr. Williams.

Jimmy smiles and says, "Thank you, Mr. Roberts." He is very happy now.

The next day, Jimmy meets his friends at the bus stop.
They are going to school. Jimmy usually goes to school by
bus with them.

"Come on, Jimmy. Let's get on the bus," says Sarah.

Jimmy replies, "No, thanks." He has a plan. "I'm not going
to school by bus today. I'm going in my wheelchair. I must
be strong for the race."

"Okay," says Sarah.

"I'll race you to school," says Jimmy.

"Ha, ha, that's funny, Jimmy," says Sarah. "See you at school."

It is very hard work but he tries and tries. He wants to be strong for the race.

"Come on, Jimmy," Sarah shouts from the bus.

Jimmy goes all the way to school in his wheelchair.

The big day is here. It is Sports Day, today. Many people are at Bayview Sports Stadium. They are having a good time. Some people are getting ready for the races. Some people are racing.

Soon the 800 meter race will start. Jimmy is in his racing wheelchair. He looks very strong. He feels strong.

"Are you ready, Anthony?" asks Jimmy.

"Yes. I'm ready," says Anthony. "Umm . . . that's a great wheelchair, Jimmy!"

Jimmy says, "Thanks, Anthony. Good luck."

"You, too," says Anthony.

"I'll wait for you at the finish line," says Jimmy.

"No. I'll wait for *you*," says Anthony. He laughs. They both want to win.

Mr. Williams starts the race. Everybody watches them start. Jimmy starts slowly. His wheelchair is slow at the start. The runners are faster than Jimmy. Jimmy is last. But Jimmy is very strong. His wheelchair is going faster and faster, now.

Anthony is a very fast runner. He thinks, "I'm winning the race!"

Soon, Jimmy is going very fast. He's pushing his wheelchair very hard, but he is still last.

"Go, Jimmy. Go!" shouts Sarah.

"Yes. Go, Jimmy. Go!" he thinks. "I can win this race. I know I can! I can!"

Mark says, "Go, Anthony. Go! You're going to win!"

Jimmy hears Mark. "No, Anthony's not going to win," he thinks. "*I'm* going to win!"

Some racers are tired, they are running slowly. Jimmy catches them.

Jimmy is going really fast now because he is strong.
He is trying very hard. "Faster! Faster!" he thinks.
"Go, Jimmy. Go!" shouts Sarah.
Soon Jimmy catches more runners. He is in third place.
He is getting nearer to Anthony.
"I'm catching Anthony," he thinks. "200 meters to go!
I must win."
Anthony looks back at Jimmy behind him. He's a little
worried. "Wow, Jimmy's fast! I must win! I can't be
second! Go, Anthony. Go!" he thinks.

Jimmy is still in third place. He's going faster.
The other runners are very surprised by Jimmy.
Now he is second.
"Go, Jimmy. Go!" shouts Sarah. "You're going to
win, Jimmy! Go! Go!"
"I must win!" thinks Jimmy. "I must win!"
But Jimmy does not win the race. He comes second.
Anthony is the winner.

"Good job, Anthony!" says Jimmy.

Mr. Williams says, "Great race, Jimmy! You're very fast."

Jimmy replies, "Of course! I'm in this wheelchair every day. That's why I'm strong."

"Second place is very good, Jimmy!" says Sarah.

"But first place is better," he says. "I want to be first! Next year I will *win*!"